Country
Style

Country Style

Home decorating the country way

Stewart and Sally Walton

southwater

This edition is published by Southwater

Distributed in the UK by
The Manning Partnership
251–253 London Road East
Batheaston
Bath BA1 7RL
UK
tel. (0044) 01225 852 727
fax. (0044) 01225 852 852

Distributed in Australia by
Sandstone Publishing
Unit 1, 360 Norton Street
Leichhardt
New South Wales 2040
Australia
tel. (0061) 2 9560 7888
fax. (0061) 2 9560 7488

Distributed in the USA by
Ottenheimer Publishing
5 Park Center Court
Suite 300
Owing Mills MD 2117-5001
USA
tel. (001) 410 902 9100
fax. (001) 410 902 7210

Distributed in New Zealand by
Five Mile Press NZ
PO Box 33-1071
Takapuna
Auckland 9
New Zealand
tel. (0064) 9 4444 144
fax. (0064) 9 4444 518

Southwater is an imprint of Anness Publishing
Limited
© 1996, 2000 Anness Publishing Limited
1 3 5 7 9 10 8 6 4 2

Publisher **Joanna Lorenz**
Project editor **Clare Nicholson**
Designer **Lisa Tai**
Photography **Graham Rae**
Step-by-step photography **Mark Wood**
Additional photography **Michelle Garrett,
Lizzie Orme**
Stylist **Leean Mackenzie**

Previously published as *Creating Country Style*

Printed and bound in Singapore

Contents

Introduction

Decorating in the country style is a way of saying "Welcome", as clearly as if the word was written on your doormat. It sends out a subliminal message to everyone who enters, inviting them to kick off their shoes and put on a comfortable (but stylish!) pair of slippers. Perhaps the best part is that the actual process of creating is so much fun. Take your time and enjoy it – even the simplest projects should not be rushed. We hope that you will treat this book in the same way, exploring the first chapter and absorbing the basics, then browsing through all the different ideas before choosing the one you most fancy as your first project.

Right: *A selection of wonderfully tactile country pieces, all hand-crafted in the traditional way.*

Creating Country Style

You do not have to live in the countryside in order to want to decorate your home in the country style. People who live in rural areas are often less likely to seek a deliberate country look than those of us who live in towns and cities, where we feel a strong pull towards the romantic country idyll. In our imaginary countryside, fields of corn rustle in the breeze, farmers still drive horse-drawn vehicles and wonderful smells of home baking waft from the kitchen of our dreams.

The country look has come to mean assembling and embellishing a mixture of handmade things that we no longer have the time or space to make for ourselves. Hand-hooked rugs, perfectly stitched quilts, knitting, embroidery and appliqué work soften the hard edges of wooden benches and stools. Some country-style furniture is quite rough and

ready, but it combines comfortably with loved and polished antiques. It is the essence of a home evolving over many years, with no need to rush.

The lifestyle still exists, as if time has stood still, in some closed communities such as that of the Amish, who have the time to sew their famous quilts by hand, keeping everything plain in accordance with their beliefs. They still manage to combine breathtaking colours with exquisite simplicity to make some of the most sought-after textiles and fabrics in the world. The Shakers were also inspired by religion and

Above: *These painted panels have been treated with antiquing wax.*

Left: *Clever use of tongue-and-groove and cream paint gives these ordinary shelves a kitchen dresser look.*

Above: The rustic furniture combines with the wall striping and stamping to give this hallway a Mexican country look.

now, 200 years later, almost everything they designed is revered, copied and becoming very fashionable.

Country decorating has no hard edges, colour schemes are mellow and textures are natural – comfort is paramount. New pieces of furniture sit well alongside the old as long as the colours and style are in harmony. Furniture made from reclaimed wood is very popular these days. It has the weathered, worn appeal of old timber combined with the stability and strength of something newly crafted. We recommend reclaimed timber for the furniture projects in this book.

Use it rough, with all the pitting and raised grain patterns, or plane and sand it to a smooth finish then polish with antiquing wax. This is a tinted beeswax that mellows the colour of the wood, leaving a deep sheen.

To choose fabrics with a country look, take your inspiration from quilts, rugs, tapestries and weaving. Checks, ginghams, plaids and small floral patterns are all in the country mood, as are stripes and plain fabrics in earthy or plant-dyed colours. Look at nature's colours – the colours of rust, straw, earth and pebbles, set off against a clear blue sky.

Try to see the familiar things around you in a new light. Look at the pattern on an old china plate or the colours in a favourite picture. Each time you take your inspiration from the objects you love to have around you in your home, you reinforce your own individual style. And every time you make something with your hands the experience is enriching.

Quiet concentration is refreshing as well as rewarding. We hope you will find inspiration within these pages to take the time and enjoy the projects as much as we did.

Country Palette

The country palette is rich and varied, drawing on all the natural colours that we can see around us throughout the seasons. Think of the icy greens, blues and greys of winter, the iridescent spring greens that replace them, then the riot of summer colours followed by the rich, mellow shades of autumn. This is the country palette, but it would not be advisable to throw the whole lot in together – a limited palette is the key to success.

One way to decide your colour schemes is to take them from a painting, quilt or piece of china with a definite country look that holds a particular appeal for you. Painted walls suit the look, especially when the paint is applied as a colourwash. This will give a mottled patchy effect, like dappled sunlight rather than a regular all-over coating. Colour washing is the best background to use for stencilled or stamped patterns and particularly complements any uneven texture in the wall. It is also the ideal way to build up strong, rich tones by

laying one colour over another. Try mixing your own colours, following the paint mix instructions below. This country-style colour range is designed to harmonize with antiques, natural building materials and old textiles.

Key to picture

1 Cadmium Red Light and Yellow Ochre (equal parts)

2 Cadmium Red Light

3 Cadmium Red Deep and Venetian Red (equal parts)

4 Burnt Sienna and Venetian Red (equal parts)

5 Chromium Oxide Green x 4 and Raw Sienna x 1

6 Hookers Green x 2 and Yellow Ochre x 1

7 Cobalt Blue x 3; Burnt Umber x 1; White x 1

8 Ultramarine x 2; White x 2; Raw Umber x 1

9 Raw Sienna

10 Yellow Ochre and Golden Ochre (equal parts)

11 Yellow Ochre and White (equal parts)

12 White x 6; Raw Umber x 1

Above: *This chequerboard floor design uses contrasting terracotta and green – perfect colours to remind us of the countryside. A combing technique has been used to vary the intensity of the colours and allow the wood grain to show through.*

Country Textures

The textures of textiles, such as rough and homespun cloth, sacking, woven rugs and soft knitted woollen shawls, all conjure up the comfort of a country home. Wood that is smooth planed and sanded or worn from years of use is what we expect inside the house, and weathered and bleached bare wood or peeling, naturally distressed painted wood outside.

Handmade pots with natural earth colours and glazes sit comfortably alongside the cool smoothness of decorative china pieces on a wooden shelf. Cast iron hinges and handles on painted tongue-and-groove doors provide a real contrast in textures, especially once the iron has become pitted with age.

Floors of worn flagstones or floorboards reveal paths most trodden, but if you cannot wait for this to happen naturally a bit of clever fakery with antiquing varnish and moulded resin flagstones will provide the visual effect. The country look is utilitarian, without too many fussy frills and flounces, but there is room for pretty textural contrasts in the bedroom with cotton quilts, embroidered cushions and crisply starched bed linen.

Above: *Pierced tinware looks good in a country kitchen, and this heart-shaped platter has acquired a wonderful patina with age. Combined like this, in a group with earthenware mugs and sheaves of wheat, the effect is stunning.*

Left: *A wrought-iron strap hinge supporting a painted plank door. The pitted iron against the wood provides a real contrast in textures.*

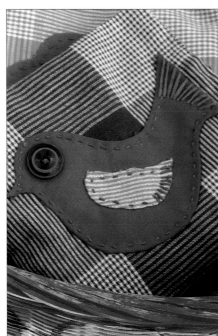

Top left: *A clever use of chicken wire. This little hanging container has been made by bending chicken wire around a wire frame.*

Bottom left: *An unusual contemporary country appliqué, using a woven background to set off a bird with a button eye.*

Right: *The texture of this hand-thrown ceramic pot sits well against the simple, plain wall surface.*

Country Materials

In the last century, before the railway arrived, all building was done with local materials. So, if you lived somewhere that had a good supply of brick, stone, timber or flint, then this is what your house was made from.

Right: Natural dyes and roughspun cotton give these Shaker-style fabrics a warm homespun quality.

Below left: Stir up summer memories with a basket filled with dried cottage garden flowers.

Below right: Reels of intensely coloured paper twine are perfect for tying up bunches of herbs or flowers. Using twine instead of string will make all the difference to a display.

Country materials come from natural sources – trees, plants, animals and the earth, but these days a lot of the goods we buy will have been manufactured in factories that have little connection with the countryside. Luckily, most country people still think locally when it comes to materials, and it is always a joy to discover a local basket weaver, wood carver or potter selling their wares in markets or at country fairs.

Choose textiles woven from wool, flax or cotton, and go for the ones

Top left: *Old kitchen implements such as wooden spoons and rolling pins should be snapped up to add authentic touches to the contemporary country kitchen.*

Top right: *A simple tin star, made into something special by hammering a dented but not pierced pattern into the back. A group of different shapes makes an eye-catching display.*

Below: *Handmade and naturally dyed papers bound together with rough twisted twine.*

with irregularities rather than smooth perfection. Loose woven or knitted throws can be used to soften chairs, hooked rag rugs are a very economical way to dispose of old clothes and gain a warm treat underfoot. Wood always feels warm, and is best oiled and beeswaxed to bring out the grain and add a delicious aroma. Quarry tiles are practical and good-looking for kitchen floors, and their warm colour suits the country palette. When in doubt always choose natural over synthetic and local over imported, and you will not go far wrong.

Motifs and Patterns

ome patterns used in country-style decorating are inspired by nature and the country life-style; flowers, the sun, trees, farm animals and birds all feature. Others have come from traditional sources like the heart, which always stands for love, or the star, which appears more in American country style than European but is a universal motif because we all live beneath the stars.

Plaid patterns and checks are a result of the weaving process. When all fabric was handmade on a loom, some threads were coloured with nat-

ural dyes made from the earth, berries and roots and then interwoven with the undyed threads. We associate the classic cream and red, blue, green or yellow checks and stripes with this style. Nowadays, when there is such a great range of patterns available, there is something particularly comforting about choosing these simple basic patterns and colour combinations for our homes.

In the same way that the weaving process limited the way cloth was patterned, most country motifs have been simplified to suit their method of

Left: *The classic geometric eight-pointed star, used here as a stencilled border but seen more often as a pieced quilt pattern.*

Above: *The pineapple was used to convey hospitality, so this stamped pineapple is the ideal motif for a placemat on the dinner table.*

Right: *This border has been hand painted on to floorboards, using a stencil for the basic shape and adding details freehand.*

Above: *The heart is one of the most popular motifs in folk art and country decorating. Its meaning as a love symbol is universally understood.*

Below: *These beautiful hand-stitched quilts have been made with traditional patterns. The basket is a symbol of generosity; the pineapples mean hospitality.*

Above: *This breakfast tablecloth is decorated with a geometric cockerel motif. It is a traditional country farmhouse motif that reminds us of the early morning.*

production. Stencils pare down motifs, concentrating the main characteristics of each shape so that it can be cut and painted effectively. Each cut-out section of a stencil needs a "bridge" to keep it attached to the rest of the design, and these give stencilled patterns and motifs their distinctive look.

Stamped patterns have a similar "cut-out" quality to stencils, but they have no bridges to interfere with basic shapes. Country painters are not slaves to convention though, and it is common to find a mixture of techniques used on a wall or piece of furniture – a simple stencilled leaf shape, for instance, with freehand veining added with the sweep of a brush.

You find the same applies in patchwork quilting and appliqué, where shapes are cut and sewn, or in tapestry and cross stitch, where the silks are worked on to a mesh backing, which makes all motifs more angular.

When looking for country motifs and patterns, choose anything that celebrates nature's bounty – sheaves of wheat, fruit, farmhouses, barns, weather vanes, farm gates, cows, sheep, horses, dogs and cats, a cockerel, geese and wild birds, traditional patterns such as stars, hearts, baskets, checks, stripes and bows. All of these can be interpreted in many different ways to create wonderful patterns in your home.

Surfaces

One of the things you notice first in a country home is that the interior decoration places equal emphasis on comfort and practicality. If people are likely to walk mud through the hall, there is no point laying a pale carpet or hanging expensive wallpaper. Instead floors are polished wood or flagstone and walls are panelled or painted. Mellowed or distressed paintwork immediately fits in with existing country furnishings and will accept wear and tear quite amiably. In this chapter we focus on interesting ways to paint interior surfaces – walls, floors and woodwork – in true country style.

Right: Pigments and stains can be stirred into easy-to-use water-based paints to create your own country colour schemes.

Country Surfaces

Country style should appear effortless and look as if it has always been there. This may sound difficult at first, but a few basic techniques will give you the confidence to relax and enjoy this very "hands on" approach to decorating your home.

The wall finishes most associated with the country look are colourwash, chalky distemper, limewash, stencilling, stippling and distressing. Colourwash is often used as the base for further decorative effects such as stencilling. When paint is washed on to a wall, it makes it appear dappled with light and shade, and even the smoothest modern wall takes on a more interesting surface texture.

Country woodwork is left natural, perhaps with a coat of varnish, or painted with matt (flat) paint, not gloss. Emulsion (latex) paint is often used on bare wood then sanded off to reveal the grain beneath. Fine-grade wire wool (steel wool) can be used

instead of sandpaper – it is less scratchy and gives a smoother finish. Another simple technique is to run a candle along the edge of a skirting board or other piece of woodwork, then apply a water-based paint over it. The wax resists the paint, giving the effect of natural wear and tear.

Stencils can be bought ready-cut, and many companies send out mail-order catalogues of their designs. You

can also cut your own designs from stencil card (cardboard) or plastic. This way you can decide on the size of the design and tailor it to suit your room, and it is much more satisfying to go through the whole process yourself – the sense of achievement is well worth the extra effort. For an unusual effect, try the Star Stencil project, in which we show how to stencil a wall with varnish, something we discoverd

Above: *The stencilling here has been done with a very light touch to blend with the mottled and dragged backgrounds. The crisp perfection of the bed linen provides a strong contrast.*

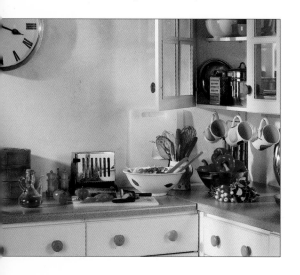

Left: *A contemporary kitchen with new units and appliances is softened by adding a diluted wash of mottled colour to the walls.*

Above: *This is formal country style with a Scandinavian theme. The flat blue background has been stamped with two similar motifs to create a dynamic background for the elegant mirrors.*

by accident one day when we splashed varnish on a painted wall.

Stamping produces a similar result to stencilling, but by the opposite method. Instead of working with a negative (the cut-away part of the stencil) you use a positive (the actual stamp), which is inked and pressed on to the surface. Stamps can be made out of foam rubber, erasers, kitchen sponges or polystyrene (styrafoam). The Horse Border is done with a stamp. As with stencils, many mail-order companies and shops now supply readymade stamps in a wide variety of designs.

All the surface finishes shown in this chapter are simple and satisfying to do. They provide the perfect background for country-style furniture and accessories.

Gingham Painted wall

✳ Gingham is, of course, the classic country-style fabric, but here this perennial favourite has been given a fresh new twist by imitating it in paint. The clever but simple technique is to cut the paint roller in half so that you can paint two stripes at the same time. For a completely different effect, try using the traditional Shaker pattern of brick red checks on a buff background.

YOU WILL NEED
- **white emulsion (latex) paint**
- **large decorator's paintbrush**
- **small foam paint roller (as sold for gloss paint)**
- **masking tape**
- **craft knife**
- **yellow emulsion (latex) paint**
- **small sponge**
- **spirit (carpenter's) level**

1 *Paint the walls with white emulsion (latex) as a base coat. Wrap a piece of masking tape around the centre of the foam part of the paint roller.*

2 *Using a craft knife, cut through the foam, using the edges of the masking tape as a guide on either side.*

3 *Peel off the masking tape with the foam attached, to leave a space in the middle. Reassemble the paint roller.*

4 *Fill the paint tray with yellow emulsion (latex) and run the paint roller through it. Starting as close to the top of the wall as possible, paint even vertical stripes. Fill in any gaps at the top or bottom with a small sponge. Leave to dry.*

5 *Paint the horizontal stripes, using a spirit (carpenter's) level to keep them straight. Focus your eyes on a point ahead and your arm will then naturally follow in a straight line.*

Star Stencil

✹ This misty blue colour scheme is ideal for a bathroom or staircase because the lower part of the wall is varnished to provide a practical wipe-clean surface. The tinted varnish deepens the colour and gives it a sheen that contrasts beautifully with the chalky distemper above. The stencil is a traditional quilting motif.

YOU WILL NEED

- **star template (see page 150)**
- **tracing paper and pencil**
- **scissors**
- **spray mount adhesive**
- **stencil card (cardboard)**
- **sharp craft knife and cutting mat**
- **soft blue distemper or chalk-based paint**
- **large decorator's paintbrushes**
- **straightedge and spirit (carpenter's) level**
- **clear satin water-based varnish**
- **Prussian blue artist's acrylic paint**

1 *Trace the star shape and cut out. Spray the back lightly with adhesive, then stick it on to the stencil card (cardboard).*

2 *Using a craft knife, cut out the star. Cut inwards from the points towards the centre so that the points stay crisp.*

➤

3 *Peel away the paper template to reveal the stencil.*

4 ▷ *Dilute the paint, if necessary, according to the manufacturer's instructions. Brush it on to the wall with sweeping, random strokes to give a colourwashed effect.*

5 ◁ *Using a straightedge and spirit (carpenter's) level, draw a pencil line across the wall at the height you want to end the varnished surface.*

6 ▷ *Tint the varnish with a squeeze of Prussian blue acrylic paint. Using a separate brush, apply this on the lower part of the wall up to the marked line.*

7 ◁ *Spray the back of the stencil lightly with adhesive and position at one end of the wall, about 5 cm (2 in) above the marked line. Stencil with the tinted varnish, using a broad sweep of the brush. Repeat along the wall, spacing the stars evenly.*

Country Wall surface

✸ Tongue-and-groove is a typical wall treatment in country cottages, larders and pantries, especially when topped with a display shelf for a collection of pretty china. Tongue-and-groove is practical as well as decorative, providing insulation and hiding uneven surfaces. Another advantage is that it is simple to hammer nails into the wood if you want to hang pictures. Most timber merchants and hardware stores sell tongue-and-groove, sometimes even in kit form.

YOU WILL NEED

- **retractable tape measure**
- **straightedge and spirit (carpenter's) level**
- **three lengths of battening, to fit your wall width**
- **hand drill**
- **wall plugs (plastic anchors)**
- **screwdriver and screws**
- **tongue-and-groove planks, to fit your wall depth – measured from skirting board (baseboard) to picture-rail height**
- **hammer**
- **panel pins (small fine nails)**
- **fine nail punch**
- **shelf brackets, enough to fit your wall width when spaced 60 cm (24 in) apart**
- **15 cm (6 in) wide shelving plank, to fit your wall width**
- **flat beading (molding), to fit your wall width**
- **saw**
- **white emulsion (latex) paint**
- **medium decorator's brush**

1 *Carefully remove any existing skirting board (baseboard), to be replaced later. Using the straightedge and spirit (carpenter's) level, mark the position for three levels of battening at the top, centre and bottom of the wall. Drill and insert the wall plugs (plastic anchors), then screw the battens in place.*

2 *Place the first tongue-and-groove plank against the wall and attach to the three battens with panel pins (nails). Check the vertical with the spirit (carpenter's) level. Tap panel pins (nails) through the inside edge of the "tongue" into the battens.*

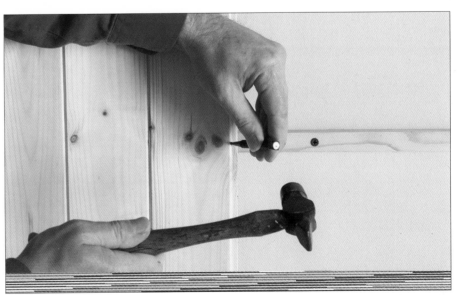

3▷ *Using a nail punch, hammer the heads of the panel pins below the surface of the wood.*

4 *Drill holes 60 cm (24 in) apart for the shelf supports so that the shelf will sit at the top of the tongue-and-groove. Screw in place, checking that they are level.*

5 *Place the shelving plank on top of the brackets. Drill holes to line up with the brackets, then screw in place from above.*

6 *Cut a piece of beading (molding) to fit between each pair of brackets. Tap in place to conceal the raw edges of the tongue-and-groove. Replace the skirting board. Paint the tongue-and-groove and shelf with white emulsion (latex) diluted 50/50 with water.*

Painted Staircase

Painting a staircase in three strong colours makes it into a central feature that will transform a room. For a co-ordinated look, repeat the colours on the walls. Gloss paint is normally used on stairs because it gives a thick, tough surface, but when it begins to chip off it looks very scruffy. Here ordinary emulsion (latex) has been used instead, painted over white primer. You can also paint directly on to bare wood – when the paint wears, the wood will show through to give the distressed finish so typical of country style.

1 *Paint the wooden staircase with white acrylic primer. Paint the wall behind the staircase with blue emulsion (latex), continuing the colour a quarter of the way across the stair treads and risers. This edge will be painted over.*

2 *Paint the banisters and side panel with mustard yellow emulsion (latex). Protect the rest of the staircase and floor with a dust sheet (tarp).*

3 *Paint the outer skirting with blue emulsion (latex), continuing the colour a quarter of the way across the stair treads and risers as in step 1.*

4 *Place strips of masking tape down the staircase, leaving an equal amount of blue paint either side. Paint the centre of the treads and risers with brick red emulsion (latex). Paint the handrail brick red, leave to dry, then add a thin yellow line.*

Stamped Horse border

✴ Add extra interest to a painted floor or wall with this simple border pattern. Cutting the stamp isn't difficult but works best if you use high-density foam, the type used for camping and exercise mats. Don't attempt to cut right through the foam the first time. Use a small paint roller to apply the paint – if you simply press the stamp into the paint, it will absorb too much. Practise first on paper before starting the border. It's very easy!

YOU WILL NEED
- **hired sanding machine and hand-held electric sander (for unpainted floors)**
- **horse template (see page 150)**
- **tracing paper and pencil**
- **spray mount adhesive**
- **square of 1 cm (½ in) thick high-density foam**
- **craft knife**
- **ruler**
- **wood stain: light blue and white**
- **medium decorator's paintbrush**
- **dark blue emulsion (latex) paint**
- **small gloss paint roller and tray**
- **clear matt (flat) hardwearing polyurethane varnish and brush**

1 *If your floor is unpainted, sand with a hired sanding machine, then finish with a hand-held electric sander.*

2 *Trace the horse motif. Spray the back lightly with adhesive, then stick it on to the piece of foam.*

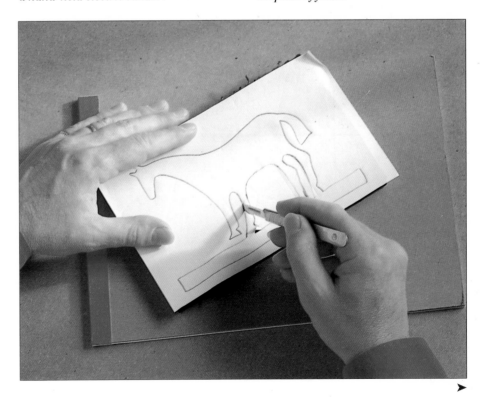

3 ▷ *Using a craft knife, "draw" a cut around the horse. Correct any sharp angles.*

➤

4 *Make another angled cut to meet the first, then pull away a thin strip of foam from the edge of the horse, revealing the outline. Cut through the full depth of foam. Peel off the paper.*

5 ▷ *Place the stamp on the floor to help determine the width of the border, a little way out from the wall.*

6 ◁ *Paint the thin strip of floor near the wall with blue wood stain. When dry, paint the border area with white wood stain. Stain the rest of the floor blue.*

7 ▷ *Pour some dark blue emulsion (latex) into a paint tray. Using a roller, apply an even coat of paint to the stamp.*

8 *Start stamping at a corner or focal point. Place the inked stamp directly on to the floor and apply even pressure. Lift off directly to avoid smudges. Change the angle slightly each time to vary the effect. Seal the floor with two coats of clear matt (flat) polyurethane varnish.*

Chequerboard Floor

✴ Painting a patterned floor may seem a daunting task, but stunning results such as this combed design will bring you endless compliments. The materials cost very little compared to laying a carpet. If the room is large, use a straight-edge to check the grid lines. A cardboard square the actual size of the finished squares will also help you to align the design. Start painting in the farthest corner and paint your way out of the room.

YOU WILL NEED
- **several pieces of thick mounting (mat) board**
- **craft knife**
- **white emulsion (latex) paint**
- **large decorator's brush**
- **retractable tape measure**
- **2.5 cm (1 in) wide masking tape**
- **long straightedge (optional)**
- **38 cm (15 in) card (cardboard) square (optional)**
- **artist's acrylic paint: terracotta and green**
- **medium decorator's paintbrush**
- **clear matt (flat) hardwearing polyurethane varnish and brush**

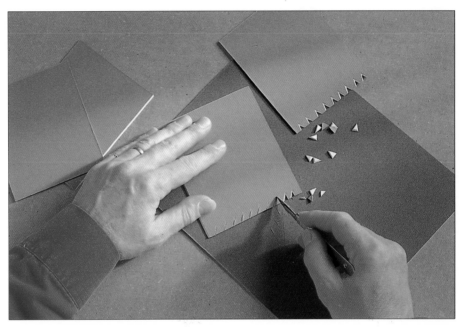

1 *Cut V-shaped "teeth" along one edge of each piece of mounting (mat) board, to make combs. The combs will soften with use.*

2 *Paint the floor with white emulsion (latex). When dry, lay masking tape all around the edge of the room.*

3 *Using a tape measure, mark 40 cm (16 in) squares on the tape. Start in the most visible corner, measuring half a square (20 cm/8 in) in each direction.*

➤

4◁ *Lay down a grid of tape lines. Use a straightedge and/or a 38 cm (15 in) card (cardboard) square, if necessary, to help keep the squares even.*

5 *Experiment on a piece of card (cardboard) to find the amount of paint most suitable for combing. Apply the paint generously on the floor, alternating the colours.*

6 *Press a comb down into the paint, wiggling it from side to side to vary the pattern. Wipe off the paint when the comb begins to clog and replace with a new comb when necessary. Leave to dry overnight, then remove the tape. Apply two coats of varnish.*

Door panel Motifs

These bold circles are reminiscent of the "hex" signs that the early Pennsylvanian Dutch settlers painted on the sides of their barns to ward off evil and protect the grain within. The geometric designs are drawn with a compass. You need a steady hand to paint in the colours, and it helps to use your spare hand as a support, either by holding your wrist or by resting one hand on the other.

YOU WILL NEED

- sage green emulsion (latex) paint
- medium decorator's paintbrushes
- pair of compasses
- pencil
- artist's acrylic paints: burnt umber, white, cadmium yellow and Indian red
- 1 cm (½ in) square-tipped paintbrush
- masking tape (optional)
- fine-tipped no. 2 lining brush
- clear matt (flat) or satin acrylic varnish

1 *Paint the door with sage green emulsion (latex). Using a pair of compasses and pencil, draw two large circles in the centre of each top panel.*

2 *Keeping the same radius measurement, draw the stylized petals. Place the compass point on the edge of the circle and make a series of arcs as shown.*

3 *Add smaller circles as shown, using the compass.*

4 ▷ *Mix a little burnt umber into some white acrylic paint. Fill in the panels, painting around the circles.*

5 *Using the square-tipped paintbrush, paint the door beading (molding) yellow. Use masking tape to give a neat edge, if you find it difficult.*

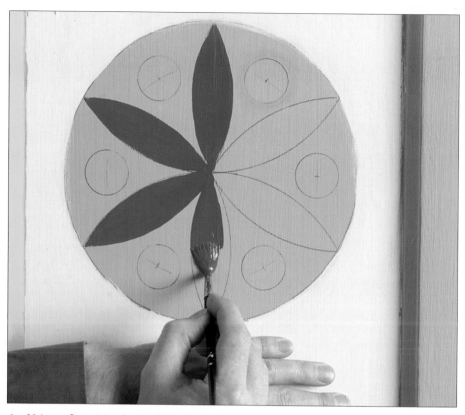

6△ *Using a fine-tipped no. 2 lining brush, carefully fill in the petal shapes in each circle. Then leave to dry.*

7 *Fill in the red dots.*

8△ *Edge the yellow beading (molding) with fine red lines. Leave to dry, then varnish, using a separate brush.*

Painted Window surround

✳ This window treatment is inspired by pargeting, a traditional technique in which wet plaster was imprinted with simple patterns. This painted version, with mock panels on either side, would make a feature of an awkward window. Experiment with thinning the paint – it should flow smoothly off the brush. Instead of a painter's mahl stick (maulstick), you can tape a small wad of cotton wool covered with lint or chamois leather to the end of a stick.

YOU WILL NEED
- **white emulsion (latex) paint**
- **artist's acrylic paints: yellow ochre and burnt umber**
- **large decorator's paintbrush**
- **ruler and pencil**
- **straightedge**
- **pair of compasses**
- **mahl stick (maul stick)**
- **no. 8 soft watercolour brush**

1 *Tint some white emulsion (latex) with yellow ochre to make a soft straw yellow. Top up with water to make a thin, milky glaze. Brush on to the wall, varying the direction of your strokes to give an uneven colour.*

2 *Measure a 10 cm (4 in) wide border around the window, using a straightedge, and draw in lightly in pencil.*

3 *Leave a gap of 15 cm (6 in), then draw a panel on either side of the window. The width of the panel should be half the width of your window. Draw a 10 cm (4 in) border inside each panel. Using a pair of compasses, draw two circles inside each panel. Draw quarter-circles in the corners.*

➤

4 *Using the card (cardboard) as a template, draw three outlines in pencil on the backing board, centred above each peg hole.*

5 ▷ *Fill in the three outlines with undiluted white emulsion (latex).*

6 *Photocopy the number templates, enlarging them to 7.5 cm (3in) high.*

7 ▷ *Using masking tape, attach a number on top of each white outline, then slip a piece of transfer paper (carbon paper) underneath.*

8 ◁ *Trace around the outline of each number in pencil. Remove the templates and transfer paper (carbon paper).*

9 ▷ *Paint each number a different colour, using a lining brush. Practise using the brush first – it helps to support your hand to keep it steady.*

10 *Using the square-tipped paintbrush, paint each peg to match the corresponding number. Glue the pegs in position.*

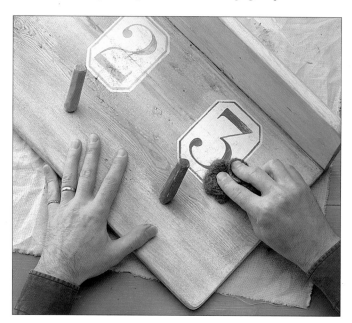

11 *Rub back the painted numbers lightly with wire wool (steel wool). Apply a coat of clear varnish or clear wax polish.*

1 2 3

Pawprint Shelves

✴ This simple paint effect is based on the traditional "pawprint" pattern – the more naive and informal it looks, the better. The decoration is applied very simply with a piece of sponge to give an all-over, random effect. This technique could be used on another piece of wooden furniture, such as a cupboard or chair.

YOU WILL NEED
- **old wooden shelf unit**
- **fine-grade sandpaper**
- **acrylic paint: golden ochre and Venetian red**
- **old white plate**
- **small decorator's brushes**
- **small piece of sea sponge**
- **pencil**
- **no. 2 lining brush**
- **PVA (white) glue**

1▷ *Sand the shelf unit.*

2◁ *Pour some golden ochre paint on to a plate. Paint the shelf unit and then leave to dry.*

3 *Add some Venetian red paint to darken the colour. Dip a small piece of sponge in the mixture and apply in spots all over the shelf unit. Leave to dry.*

➤

4 *Using a pencil, mark a line all around the top of the shelf unit. Rest the point of the pencil on the front, keeping your other fingers rigid, then run the pencil along to give an even line.*

5 ▷ *Using a lining brush, carefully go over the pencil line with Venetian red paint. Support your painting hand to keep it steady. Leave to dry.*

6 *Pour some PVA (white) glue on to a plate and mix in a brushful of Venetian red paint to make a slightly tinted glaze. The glue is milky when wet but will be clear when dry.*

7 ▷ *Using a separate brush, paint the glaze over the shelf unit. There is no need to varnish as the glue will protect the surface.*

Tartan S t o o l

✳ Simple upholstery such as this is much easier since the invention of glue guns and staple guns. Once you have mastered the technique shown here, you can move on to more ambitious projects. This project would work equally well on an upholstered chair seat. Give a favourite piece of furniture the tartan treatment, or look out for an old stool in a junk shop. If the woodwork is not painted, paint it first with a white emulsion (latex) undercoat.

YOU WILL NEED
- **upholstered stool**
- **medium-grade sandpaper**
- **emulsion (latex) paint in a colour to match your tartan fabric**
- **small decorator's paintbrush**
- **tartan fabric, to fit the upholstered stool top plus 2.5 cm (1in) all round – the fabric should not be too thick**
- **staple gun**
- **four upholstery nails**
- **hammer**
- **scissors**
- **glue gun and glue sticks**
- **upholstery braid, to fit around the bottom of the stool top plus 2.5 cm (1 in)**

1 *Rub down the woodwork with sandpaper. Paint with emulsion (latex), then drag over a dry paintbrush while the paint is still wet.*

2 *Place the tartan fabric centrally over the upholstered stool top. Using a staple gun, put a single staple in the centre of one long side. Pull the fabric taut, then staple the opposite side in the same way.*

3 *Staple the two short sides in the same way. The fabric will now be held in place by four staples.*

4 *Staple along the edge of each side, placing the row of staples close together. Leave the corners open.*

➤

5 *Mitre the fabric at the corners and flatten the folds. Secure each corner temporarily with an upholstery nail.*

6 *Trim the excess fabric, leaving just enough to turn under a small hem and cover the corners.*

7 *Staple one mitred corner flat, turning under the small hem as you go. Remove the upholstery nail. Repeat with the opposite corner, then complete the other two corners.*

8 *Heat the glue gun. Glue one end of the braid to the bottom of the stool top at one corner. Spread a line of glue along the bottom edge.*

9 *Holding the braid taut in one hand, smooth it on to the glued line with the other hand, keeping the line straight. Fold under the end of the braid at the last corner to make a neat join.*

Kitchen Clock

✳ Every country kitchen needs a traditional wall clock, and this design also incorporates a shelf for herbs and spices. If you wish, you can decorate the simple clock case with folk art borders handpainted in bright colours. Making your own clock isn't difficult. Clock faces and movements can be bought from many places that do repairs. Cut the circular opening to fit your clock face, getting the help of a local carpenter if you don't have the necessary tools.

YOU WILL NEED

- **16 mm (⅝ in) thick medium-density fibreboard or pine, cut as follows (see templates, page 151):**
- **25 cm x 25 cm (10 in x 10 in) for the clock face**
- **two pieces 47 cm x 9 cm (18½ in x 3½ in) for the sides**
- **three pieces 9 cm x 25 cm (3½ in x 10 in) for the top, bottom and shelf**
- **10.5 cm (4½ in) of 9 mm (⅜ in) dowel for the shelf rail**
- **50 cm (20 in) of small moulding to finish the top**
- **white metal clock face with Roman numerals**
- **yellow ochre emulsion (latex) paint**
- **medium decorator's brush**
- **antiquing wax**
- **soft cloth**
- **wire wool (steel wool)**
- **glue gun and glue sticks**

1 *Make the clock case, following the diagram on page 151. Paint with yellow ochre emulsion (latex) and leave to dry.*

2 *Rub in a generous coat of antiquing wax, working it well into the corners and grain (if you are using pine). Rub down the polish with wire wool (steel wool) so that the colour shows through stronger in some areas but the wax remains in the grooves and corners.*

3 *Rub the clock face with antiquing wax to mellow the colour.*

4 *Fit the clock movement to the face from behind.*

5 *Press the hands on to the spindle. Using a glue gun, stick the clock face to the inside of the case – mark the vertical centre point on the back of the clock face to help you position the numbers.*

Fabrics

ountry fabrics are natural rather than man-made – muslin, calico, canvas, textured homespun linen and, of course, cotton. Floral prints, stripes, checks and plaids complement country furniture and surfaces perfectly. The tradition of making patchwork quilts and rag rugs continues today, sometimes giving a new interpretation to an old design. Appliqué, cross stitch embroidery, knitting and quilting are all part of the country style – all made with love and made to last. Create a nostalgic country mood by using a range of fabrics that are full of associations with nature and folklore.

Right: *Gingham checks, striped cottons and chequered bedspreads all improve with age. This pile of country fabrics looks far too good to hide away in a cupboard. Folded and stacked on open shelves, household linens make an appealing display.*

Country Fabrics

Above: *Try embroidering simple waffle-weave cotton tea towels. This tea towel has been embellished with a Danish-style cross motif.*

Left: *Woven stripes in coarse cotton make ideal upholstery fabric for a whole range of country furnishings.*

The country fabrics that we recognize today are a cultural blend of patterns and designs from many different parts of the world. The overall country look combines the warm generosity of places such as Provence, Tuscany and Greece with the simplicity of the Shaker and Amish communities, plus a dash of medieval, Celtic and oriental spice. The unifying factor is that all these fabrics were originally made and decorated by hand, even if today they are printed and produced in factories.

In this chapter, we use a potato to print an all-over pattern on the Clover Leaf Tablecloth and a piece of sponge to print a traditional appliqué design on the Stamped Throw. Both are done with water-based inks, which are much more pleasant to work with than oil-based inks.

The sewing projects include a quick-and-easy Squared Patchwork Quilt, stitched on a sewing machine, and a hand-stitched Appliqué Window Quilt. The hand-stitching is far more time-consuming but it is very satisfying and relaxing to do, and the irregularity of the stitched outlines adds greatly to the quilt's charm. Iron-on wadding (batting) makes the whole business of making up a quilt much quicker and simpler than it used to be.

The Hooked Rag Rug is the traditional family way to pass the long winter's evenings, and a wonderful way to recycle old clothes. Another unusual floor covering is the Stars-and-Stripes Floor Cloth, made of painted canvas. Given several coats of varnish, these floor cloths are incredibly hardwearing. If you have never worked a sewing machine or tried

Above: *Stripes used horizontally instead of vertically can make narrow windows appear wider. Any fabric left over from new curtains can be used for chair skirts or cushions for a co-ordinated look.*

your hand at embroidery before, several ideas in this chapter are very simple. The Cross Stitch Napkins is an ideal project to start with.

Colours do not always have to co-ordinate because country style is often an eclectic mix of patterns and colours. Fabrics and patterns are often more appealing when they have faded over time, and the aim should be to re-create this warm, comfortable and, above all, practical look.

Stars and stripes Floor cloth

✴ Varnished floor cloths were introduced by the early American settlers, who recycled the canvas sails that had carried them to the New World and painted them to imitate European carpets. Make this bright floor cloth to cover most of the room or just as a small mat – artist's suppliers sell canvas in a wide range of sizes. It is available pre-primed or you can prime it yourself. Each coat of varnish you apply will add years to the floor cloth's life.

YOU WILL NEED

- natural-coloured artist's canvas, size as required
- ruler and pencil
- craft knife
- 5 cm (2 in) double-sided carpet tape
- white acrylic primer (optional)
- medium decorator's brush
- masking tape
- acrylic paint: scarlet, cobalt blue and white
- old white plate
- star template (see page 153)
- tracing paper and pencil
- spray mount adhesive
- stencil card (cardboard)
- cutting mat
- stencil brush
- clear or antique tinted matt (flat) polyurethane varnish and brush

1 *Draw a 10 cm (4 in) border on all four sides of the back of the canvas. Using a craft knife, cut across the corners as shown.*

2 *Stick double-sided tape along the border line. Peel off the backing, then fold over the raw edge.*

3 *If your canvas is unprimed, apply two coats of acrylic primer.*

4 *Mark vertical stripes 7.5 cm (3 in) wide down the canvas. Outline alternating stripes with masking tape.*

5 *Paint alternating stripes with scarlet acrylic paint.*

➤

6 Leave to dry, then peel off the masking tape.

7▽ Trace the star template. Spray the back lightly with adhesive and stick on to stencil card (cardboard). On a cutting mat, cut out the template.

8◁ Place the stencil on a white stripe, about 5 cm (2 in) from one end of the canvas. Using a stencil brush, apply blue paint sparingly, working inwards from the points of the star. Wipe the back of the stencil to avoid smudging. Space the stars about 10 cm (4 in) apart along all the white stripes.

9△ Repeat with white paint on the red stripes, positioning the white stars to fall halfway between the blue stars.

10◁ Apply at least three coats of varnish. Use an antique tinted varnish if you wish to mellow the bright colours.

Stamped Throw

✳ A casually draped throw is one of the essentials of country style, softening hard edges and hiding a multitude of sins. This floral design is adapted from an old appliqué quilt and has been translated into three stamps. Copy the colours shown here or adapt them to suit your own colour scheme. Special block-printing fabric ink in a wide range of colours is available from art and craft suppliers. Slightly textured fabric gives extra interest, but it should not be too irregular.

YOU WILL NEED
- **old blanket**
- **drawing pins (thumb tacks)**
- **three templates (see page 153)**
- **tracing paper and pencil (optional)**
- **spray mount adhesive**
- **1 cm (½ in) thick high-density foam**
- **craft knife and masking tape**
- **palette knife**
- **sheet of glass**
- **water-based block-printing fabric inks in two or more colours**
- **small gloss paint roller**
- **square of off-white cotton fabric, to the size required**
- **sewing machine and matching thread**

1 *Pin the blanket to a tabletop, using drawing pins, to allow some "give" when you stamp. Trace or photocopy the templates. Spray the back lightly with adhesive and stick on to three roughly cut pieces of foam.*

2 *Cut out the shapes with a craft knife, using sweeping hand movements rather than lots of small cuts. Use the craft knife to "draw" around each shape, then bend the foam to open the cut and pull away the excess foam.*

3◁ *Peel off the templates. Make a small handle out of masking tape for the back of each stamp.*

4▽ *Using a palette knife on a sheet of glass, mix two or more printing ink colours to give subtle tones.*

5 *Run the paint roller through the ink and apply an even coating of colour to the straight border stamp.*

6 *Machine stitch a hem around all four edges of the fabric, then place it on the blanket. Position the stamp near one corner and apply even pressure. Lift off directly so as not to smudge the colour. Stamp squares all over the fabric.*

7◁ *Apply paint to the centre motif and place in the middle of a square, positioning it by eye to give a natural, hand-printed look. Repeat with the other squares.*

8▽ *Wash the glass and paint roller, then change to the second ink colour. Add four leaf shapes to each square – don't worry if they overlap the border. Leave to dry.*

Appliqué *Window quilt*

✳ The idea of a window quilt is practical as well as decorative. It is particularly good in the winter time as it keeps out draughts at night. The inspiration for this appliqué coffee cup design comes from an old American quilt pattern originally published in Chicago in the 1940s. The sentiment is hospitality, which makes it very welcoming in the kitchen. This quilt is hung very simply from curtain clips.

YOU WILL NEED

- two coffee cup templates (see page 154)
- tracing paper and pencil
- spray mount adhesive
- card (cardboard)
- craft knife
- cutting mat or large piece of thick card (cardboard)
- fine black felt-tipped pen
- 50 cm (½ yd) each of cotton fabric in mid-blue, red-brown and olive green
- scissors
- dressmaker's pins
- pre-washed natural calico, to fit the size of your window frame plus 5 cm (2 in) all round
- sewing needle and thread
- thin iron-on wadding (batting), the same size as the calico
- iron
- mid-blue cotton fabric, 7.5 cm (3 in) larger all around than the calico
- curtain clips

1 *Trace both coffee cup templates. Spray the back lightly with adhesive and stick on to card (cardboard).*

2 *Cut out the shapes, using a craft knife and a cutting mat or large piece of card (cardboard).*

3 *Using a felt-tipped pen, draw around the large cup shape on to each fabric colour. Draw about six cups at a time.*

4 ▷ *Place the smaller shape inside each outline. Draw the shape indicated by the fold lines and also the snip lines.*

➤

5 *Cut out the large coffee cup shapes.*

6▽ *Snip up to the fold line as marked on the curved edges.*

7◁ *Pin the coffee cups to the calico fabric, alternating the colours and spacing them evenly.*

8▷ *Using your thumbnail to crease the fabric, turn under a small hem around each shape.*

9◁ *Slip stitch around each shape, using the needle to tuck in untidy edges. Bring the needle up through the shape and directly down into the calico, then bring it up further along for the next stitch. Any irregularity is part of its charm.*

To make up the quilt:

Iron the wadding (batting) to the back of the calico, placing a cloth under the iron. Lay the blue backing fabric out flat and centre the quilt right side up on top. Fold the blue fabric over on all sides to make a border. Turn under the raw edges and slip stitch to the edge of the quilt. Attach curtain clips to the top.

Rooster Cushion

✴ The handsome cockerel is a favourite motif in folk art all over the world. Its proud shape has been used to decorate everything from church spires to tin trays. This combination of gingham fabric and roosters is pure country style. The process used is photocopy transfer, which is done by photocopy shops that print T-shirts. The print is washable, but avoid direct contact with a hot iron.

YOU WILL NEED
- rooster image (see page 153)
- scissors
- A3 (12in x 16in) sheet of white paper
- spray mount adhesive
- 50 cm (½ yd) beige cotton fabric
- 40 cm x 40 cm (16 in x 16 in) square of blue-and-beige gingham cotton fabric
- dressmaker's pins
- sewing machine and matching thread
- 38 cm (15 in) square cushion pad

1 *Photocopy the rooster image five times. Cut out the shapes roughly as shown.*

2 *Arrange the photocopies on the sheet of paper. Spray the back of each image with adhesive and stick in place.*

3 *Cut a 30 cm x 30 cm (12 in x 12 in) square of beige fabric and take it and the design to a photocopy shop. Ask them to make a transfer, which should also be trimmed to make a square. The transfer should be centred on the fabric square.*

4 *Turn under a small hem all around the printed fabric. Place on the right side of the gingham fabric, in the centre. Pin in place, then machine stitch.*

5 *Cut two beige cotton backing pieces 40 cm x 30 cm (16 in x 12 in). Stitch a hem on one long edge of each piece. Right sides together, place both pieces on the cushion front so that they align with the front at either side and overlap in the middle.*

6 *Pin then stitch, adjusting the height of the needle if necessary to stitch through the four layers in the centre.*

7▷ *Clip across the corners. Turn the cushion cover right side out and insert the cushion pad.*

Cross stitch Napkin

✳ Goodlooking cross stitch relies on the stitches being regular, so checked or gingham fabric makes an ideal ready-made grid. This very easy project is an ideal place to start if you have not done much embroidery before. The cotton fabric should be quite thick and coarsely woven, with a thick embroidery thread to match. Cross stitch will also add a handmade quality to a set of bought table napkins.

YOU WILL NEED

for four napkins

- **1 m (1 yd) heavyweight checked cotton fabric**
- **dressmaker's scissors**
- **dressmaker's pins**
- **needle and thread**
- **sewing machine and matching thread**
- **embroidery scissors**
- **stranded embroidery cotton (floss), in bright contrast colour**
- **embroidery needle**

1 *Cut the fabric into four rectangles 35 cm x 48 cm (14 in x 19 in). Turn under the raw edge on each side, then fold over again to make a narrow hem. Pin and tack (baste).*

2 *Machine stitch with matching thread, using straight or zigzag stitch.*

3 *Cut a length of embroidery thread double the width of the first napkin. Thread the embroidery needle, using all six strands, and knot the end. Leaving a blank row of checks, start at one end of a row of checks, with the knot on the reverse side. Make diagonal stitches across alternate squares to the end of the row. Finish with a neat double stitch.*

4 *Re-thread the needle as before, then work back along the same row, crossing over each diagonal stitch. Repeat to give a pattern of three cross stitch rows at both ends of each napkin.*

Squared Patchwork quilt

✷ This is the most basic of all patchwork patterns. It is quickly made on a sewing machine and really can be completed in a day! The fabrics used here have been chosen to give a restrained Shaker look. For a completely different result, use bright primary colours or a mix of small-patterned fabrics. Old country quilts often used recycled fabrics, so you could make a "memory" quilt out of your children's favourite outgrown clothes.

You will need

for a single bed-size quilt

- **1 m (1 yd) each of two different cotton fabrics**
- **tape measure**
- **dressmaker's scissors**
- **sewing machine and matching thread**
- **2 m (2 yd) medium-weight iron-on wadding (batting)**
- **iron**
- **brushed cotton single bed sheet**
- **50 cm (½ yd) contrast cotton fabric**
- **dressmaker's pins**
- **needle and matching thread**

1 *Cut an equal number of 19 cm (7½ in) squares in each fabric.*

2 *Machine stitch the squares together in rows, alternating the two fabrics. There should be nine squares in each row, starting alternate rows with the opposite colour. Make six rows altogether.*

3 *Stitch the rows together, aligning the squares.*

4 ▷ *Lay the wadding (batting) out flat with the patchwork right side up on top. Trim the wadding and reserve. Iron the patchwork, bonding the two together.*

5 *Lay patchwork right side up on top of the sheet. Trim sheet to same size. Pin around the edge, then machine stitch.*

6▽ *Measure around the quilt, then cut enough 7.5 cm (3 in) wide strips of contrast fabric to make the edging.*

7◁ *Fold each strip in half, right side out. Iron the fold.*

8 ▷ *Cut strips of wadding (batting) 2.5 cm (1 in) wide. Push right inside the folded fabric strips, then iron both sides together.*

9◁ *Open out each strip and stitch to the front of the quilt as shown.*

10▽ *Fold the edging to the back of the quilt. Turn under a small hem and pin, enclosing all the raw edges.*

➤

11 *At the corners, enclose the side edging strips in the top and bottom edging strips.*

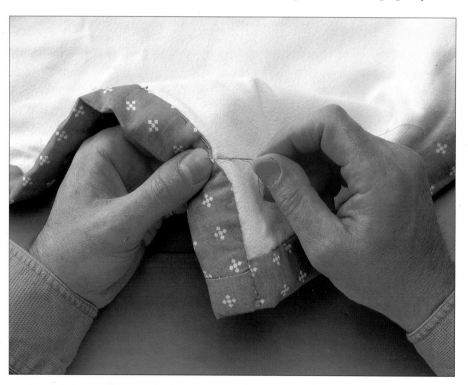

12 *Slip stitch the edging to the back of the quilt, using small neat stitches.*

Clover leaf Tablecloth

✳ This fresh four-leaf clover pattern is done very simply with a potato print. The cut potato exudes a starchy liquid that blends into the ink and adds translucence. The best fabric to print on is 100% cotton, pre-washed to remove any glaze or stiffener. The result should look handprinted, so don't despair if the edge of the potato picks up colour and prints it occasionally – it will add energy and life to the pattern. If you take a short break, place the potato in iced water and dry with kitchen paper (paper towel).

YOU WILL NEED:

- old blanket
- drawing pins (thumb tacks)
- medium-size fresh potato
- sharp knife and cutting board
- small artist's paintbrush
- craft knife
- sharp kitchen knife
- leaf green water-based block printing fabric ink (or standard primary colours: yellow, blue and red)
- sheet of glass
- palette knife
- small gloss paint roller
- white 100% cotton fabric, pre-washed and ironed, to fit your table
- sewing machine (optional) and matching thread

1 *Pin the blanket to the tabletop, using drawing pins (thumb tacks) – this allows some "give" when you apply pressure. Cut through the potato in one smooth movement to give a flat surface.*

2 *Practise painting the clover leaf on paper, copying the pattern freehand. When you are confident, paint the shape on the potato.*

3 *Cut carefully around the shape, using a craft knife. Use smooth, flowing movements to avoid jagged edges. Cut around the internal shapes. Scoop out the potato flesh with the end of the knife blade.*

4 *Cut away the waste potato to a depth of about 6 mm (¼ in).*

5 *Using a kitchen knife, trim the potato into a square. Cut a groove all around, about halfway down – this will make it easier to hold.*

6▷ *If you are using standard colours, mix 2 parts green, 1 part blue, ¼ red. Or use ready-mixed leaf green.*

7◁ *Blend the primary colours (if using) thoroughly on a sheet of glass, using a palette knife.*

8▷ *Run the paint roller through the ink until it is thoroughly coated.*

9 *Apply an even coating of ink to the potato stamp.*

10▷ *Lay the prepared fabric on the blanket and print the pattern at random. Re-ink the potato after every two printings to vary the intensity of the colour. Leave the finished fabric to dry, then hem the edges by hand or machine. Make matching napkins the same way.*

Hooked Rag rug

Rag rugs were originally a way of recycling old clothes to make soft, warm furnishings, but some of those that have survived are also works of art. The women who made them often used domestic objects such as dinner plates to make simple designs. You can trim the loops to give an even pile or leave the looped effect – both are traditional. You will get a better result if you use all wool fabrics, as they resist dirt and are comfortable underfoot. Tweed and blanket fabrics are ideal. It is a good idea to wash the fabrics first in hot water to felt the wool and give a firmer texture for cutting into strips.

YOU WILL NEED

- **coarse-weave hessian (burlap), to the finished size required plus 5 cm (2 in) all around**
- **fine black felt-tipped pen**
- **sewing needle and thread**
- **large-eyed darning needle and string**
- **wooden rugmaker's frame**
- **assortment of old woollen fabrics**
- **large scissors**
- **rug hook**

1 *Draw the outline of the rug size on the hessian (burlap), using a felt-tipped pen. Fold under a 5 cm (2 in) border all around and tack (baste).*

2 *Draw a simple design, either abstract or with stylized plants and animals.*

3 *Using string and the needle, wrap the hessian (burlap) around one end of the frame and secure with a running stitch. Repeat at other end. Assemble the frame.*

4◁ *Lace the sides of the hessian (burlap) to the frame, pulling it taut.*

5▽ *Cut the woollen fabrics as straight as possible into strips 6 mm–1 cm (¹⁄₄ in– ¹⁄₂ in) wide, depending on the strength of each fabric. Group the fabrics in colours.*

6 *Fold the first strip of fabric in half. Hold between thumb and forefinger underneath the hessian (burlap) and hook to the surface with the other hand. (The photo shows the fabric underside.)*

7 *Pull up the strip to make a loop of about 1 cm (½ in).*

8 *Push the hook back down into the hessian (burlap) a few threads further along the design and repeat.*

9 *Spacing each loop depends on the width and thickness of the fabric strips, and it will come with practice.*

10 *Bring the ends of each strip to the surface and trim. Continue to hook the design, changing colour as necessary.*

11 *When complete, remove the rug from the frame. To bind the border, fold strips of plain fabric over the edge. Stitch in place, hiding the stitches in the ragwork.*

Accessories

In country style, accessories are useful rather than purely ornamental. This does not mean that they cannot be painted or decorated to look attractive, quite the contrary. Accessories are the finishing touch that makes all the difference between a room that has no individual character and one that feels part of a home. A collection of unusual and interesting objects does not arrive all at once but evolves over a period of time, and each treasure has its own story to tell. Visiting antique stalls, shops and fairs on a regular basis will soon reap results.

Right: *The best country accessories usually look worn and loved, like this billy can, which looks perfect alongside the wire-work baskets and kitchen tools.*

Country Accessories

Once you have transformed your home with country-style paint finishes, furniture, flooring and fabrics, it is time to add the finishing touches. The accumulation of "finds" that add personality to a home does take time, and it should be a gradual process: it often depends on your being in the right place at the right time. An unlimited supply of money would buy you folk-art treasures and an interior-designed country look, but you would certainly miss out on the pleasure of making your own accessories.

There are projects in this chapter to suit most talents and skills, whether your talent lies with a needle and thread, carpenter's tools or paint-brushes. We show how household objects such as buckets and laundry baskets can add pattern and colour as well as being useful for mundane practicalities. If you look at domestic folk art, everything was considered

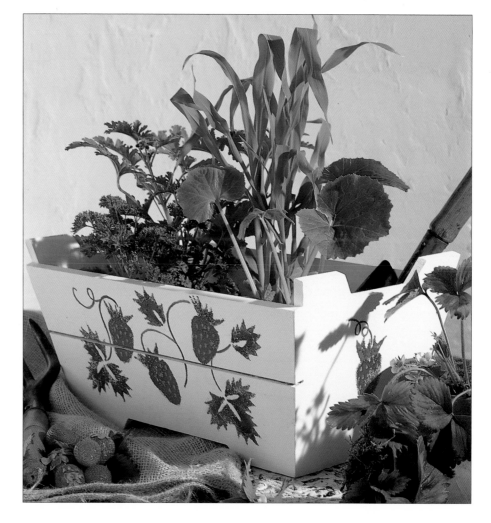

worthy of decoration. In the narrow-boats that carried coal and other heavy goods on the English canals, every jug, bowl and tray was richly ornamented with colourful paint-work. It is very satisfying to put to daily use something you have made or painted yourself.

Some of the projects require basic woodwork techniques. They can all be made on the kitchen table, but if you are not very experienced at wood-work you could perhaps find a friendly carpenter to cut the pieces for you to assemble and paint. A local carpenter may also use reclaimed

Above: *A fresh coat of white paint and stencilled strawberries have been used here to give a dull window box a country garden look.*

Left: *A rescued crate stencilled with grapevines and lined with straw makes a perfect nesting place for a collection of wine.*

timber such as old pine floorboards. It is really worth using for its character and colour. An ideal woodwork project to start with is the Framed Chalkboard. After this, try The Knife Box. It is a very traditional kitchen accessory, painted to look authentically old.

Baskets, bottles and china can all be given the country treatment, often very simply indeed. Don't be too precise about matching accessories to your existing furnishings – in this style of decorating, individual touches and character are far more important than co-ordination.

Above: *Stunning but simple, this cross stitch patterned peg bag will brighten up your washing line and relieve the wash-day blues.*

Right: *The tradition of painting household objects such as this watering can goes back a long way. Use muted colours and traditional patterns to create folk art of your own.*

Stencilled Bucket

✴ Turn an ordinary bucket into a stylish garden accessory with two cans of spray paint and a simple stencil. This pretty decoration is based on an old design discovered on the original stencilled walls in a Rhode Island house. Spray paint dries very quickly if you use it sparingly. Repeat the flower design four times around the side of the bucket.

You will need
- **flower and border templates (see page 154)**
- **tracing paper and pencil (optional)**
- **spray mount adhesive**
- **stencil card (cardboard)**
- **craft knife**
- **cutting mat or thick card (cardboard)**
- **spray paint in bright green and yellow**
- **galvanized or enamel bucket**
- **masking tape**
- **scrap paper**

1 *Trace or photocopy the templates. Spray the back lightly with adhesive and stick them on to stencil card (cardboard). Carefully cut out the shapes, using a craft knife and cutting mat or thick card (cardboard). Peel off the paper templates.*

2 *In a well-ventilated area, spray the bucket with green spray paint. Leave to dry thoroughly.*

3 *Spray the back of the flower stencil lightly with adhesive. Position the stencil on the side of the bucket.*

4 *Using masking tape, attach scrap paper around the stencil. Spray the stencil lightly with yellow paint. Lift off carefully when dry to the touch and re-position. Spray the borders in the same way.*

Rolling pin Holder

✳ This clever little device will give your rolling pin a place of its own on the kitchen wall, decorative as well as out of the way. Instead of purchasing a roll of wire, you can recycle two wire coathangers. Practise bending the wire before you start to master making smooth curves rather than sharp angles.

YOU WILL NEED

• **roll of 2 mm (¹⁄₁₀ in) wire**
• **wire-cutters and pliers (combined)**
• **screwdriver**
• **fine brass picture-hanging wire**

1 *Cut two lengths of wire 75 cm (30 in) each. Take one length, find the middle and bend it around a screwdriver to make a loop. Turn the screwdriver to twist the two halves of wire together six times.*

2 *Using the pliers, curl the two ends of the wire forwards.*

3▽ *Twist the second length of wire into a heart shape – bend it sharply in the middle, then bring the ends down in opposite directions so that they cross over. Curl the ends.*

4 *Using short lengths of brass wire, bind the two lengths together at the points shown. Place your rolling pin between the curled hooks to judge the width needed.*

Framed Memories

✳ Buy readymade box frames and give them the country treatment with a simple paint finish. Fill each frame with a miniature collection based on a particular holiday or theme – autumn leaves, pressed flowers or a seaside collection of pebbles, shells and driftwood. Mix textures and shapes, perhaps including an entrance ticket from a day out.

YOU WILL NEED
- **set of deep, square box frames**
- **masking tape**
- **acrylic paint: sky blue, brick red and dark green**
- **small decorator's paintbrush**
- **fine-grade sandpaper**
- **shellac and brush**
- **collection of natural objects**
- **glue gun and sticks**

1 *Stick masking tape around the edge of the glass of each frame to protect it from the paint. Paint the frame, choosing a colour to suit your collection.*

2 *When dry, rub with sandpaper to reveal the grain.*

3 *Apply a coat of shellac to mellow the colour of the paint. When dry, peel off the masking tape.*

4 *Paint the backing card (cardboard) with shellac.*

5 *Arrange the design on the backing card (cardboard), then glue in place. Leave to dry, then assemble the frame.*

Beaded Jug cover

✳ This is a simplified and modernized version of the intricate crochet and beadwork covers that were once a feature of every country pantry. Stitching through a paper pattern works very well because the stitches perforate the paper, making it very easy to tear off later. You can use a sewing machine, if you prefer.

YOU WILL NEED
- **jug cover template (see page 157)**
- **ruler and pencil**
- **thin paper**
- **scissors**
- **25 cm (¼ yd) white net (tulle)**
- **dressmaker's pins**
- **needle and matching thread**
- **50 cm (½ yd) gingham bias binding**
- **sewing machine (optional)**
- **eight heavy beads, in bright colours**

1 *Trace the jug cover template on to the thick paper and cut out. Repeat with the thin paper.*

2 *Fold the net to make a double layer. Pin the paper pattern to the net with a single pin. Stitch around the edge of the paper. Cut away the excess net.*

3 *Stitch one edge of the bias binding around the octagon, with the paper still in place. Pull away the paper pattern.*

4 *Fold the bias binding over to the other side of the net and stitch around the edge.*

5 *Space the beads evenly around the cover. Stitch to the bias binding, using a double loop of thread. Leave about 2.5 cm (1 in) drop of thread between each bead and the binding, then twist the end of the thread around this several times before fastening it off in the binding.*

Bay Wreath

Bunches of herbs hang in every self-respecting country kitchen, but this lovely wreath makes them into a decorative feature. The frame of the wreath is simply made from a recycled wire coathanger, which of course makes it very easy to hang up. Green tape and gardening string are both available from florists or garden centres.

YOU WILL NEED
- **wire coathanger**
- **green tape**
- **gardening string**
- **scissors**
- **sprigs of bay leaves**
- **wide green gingham ribbon**

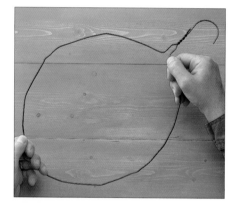

1 *Pull the coathanger into a circle with your hands, leaving the hanging hook as it is.*

2 *Bind the hook with green tape.*

3◁ *Using gardening string, tie sprigs of bay leaves on to the wire frame. Gradually build up a regular bushy shape.*

4▽ *Cut five lengths of ribbon and tie on to the wreath in simple bows.*

Cornucopia Wreath

✴ This style of wreath started in Scandinavia as a Christmas decoration, hung on the front door to welcome guests. Any mixture of nuts, herbs and spices can be used. For the base, use cuttings from a vine or similar plant, such as honeysuckle. Or ready-made natural wreath bases are available from some florists.

YOU WILL NEED

- vine cuttings or ready-made natural wreath base
- gardening string
- pliers
- gardening wire
- PVA (white) glue and brush
- old plate
- walnuts
- offcuts (scraps) of plaid or gingham fabric
- dried chillies
- small wicker baskets
- bay leaves
- dried apple rings
- cinnamon sticks

1 *Bend some of the longer cuttings into a circle and tie securely with string.*

2 *Weave more cuttings around the circle to make a solid base.*

3 *Cut short lengths of wire, dip in glue, then poke the ends into the walnut shells. Leave to dry.*

4 *Tear the fabric into strips. The frayed edges will give a homespun look.*

5 *Tie bunches of chillies together with string (don't rub your eyes!), then tie a fabric bow above each bunch. Twist several walnut wires together to make bunches, adding more bows. Pack the baskets with bay leaves and tie string on to the handles.*

6 *Tie all these objects on to the wreath. Fill the gaps with bunches of apple rings and cinnamon sticks, also tied with string.*

7 *Tie a loop of fabric at the top of the wreath for hanging.*

Decoy Birds

※ Originally wooden birds were made for the practical purpose of deceiving real birds to fly down before the hunter's gun. Today decoy birds are very collectable and also very expensive, so it is well worth making your own. These colourful little birds are sawn from an old plank. The rustic effect is enhanced by using a piece of rough weathered wood for the base.

YOU WILL NEED
- **bird templates (see page 156)**
- **tracing paper and pencil**
- **thin card (cardboard)**
- **scissors**
- **fine black felt-tipped pen**
- **floorboard or other piece of reclaimed timber**
- **clamp**
- **bradawl (awl)**
- **keyhole saw**
- **hand drill and 7 mm (⅜ in) bit**
- **1 m (38 in) of 7 mm (⅜ in) dowelling**
- **small hacksaw**
- **piece of driftwood or rough weathered wood**
- **artist's acrylic paints: red, yellow, dark green, dark brown, white and black**
- **small decorator's paintbrush**
- **old white plate**
- **medium artist's paintbrush**
- **fine-grade sandpaper**
- **PVA (white) glue**
- **clear matt (flat) varnish and brush (optional)**

3▷ *Clamp the board to a solid surface. With a bradawl (awl), make a hole at the edge of the first shape. Insert the blade of a keyhole saw through the hole and saw around the marked line. Repeat for the other birds.*

1 *Trace the templates and transfer on to thin card (cardboard). Cut out with scissors.*

2 *Using a felt-tipped pen, draw around each bird shape on to the floorboard or piece of reclaimed timber.*

➤

4 *Drill a hole in the bottom centre of each bird.*

5 *Cut the dowelling into five pieces, three 20 cm (8 in) long and two 18 cm (7 in) long.*

6 *Drill five holes in the piece of driftwood or rough wood, spacing them far enough apart for the birds to sit comfortably.*

7 *Paint the birds, each in a different colour. Leave to dry.*

8 *Add beaks and eyes in black paint. Leave to dry.*

9 *Rub over the paint with sandpaper to reveal the wood along the edges of each bird.*

10 ◁ *Glue the pieces of dowelling into the holes in the base. Glue the birds on top to make an attractive group. If desired, apply a coat of varnish.*

Collage Tree of Life

✹ The Tree of Life is a favourite subject for folk artists working in many different media. Here we have used a collage of watercolour scraps to make a very individual framed picture. Templates are supplied for the main shapes, but the essential character of the picture lies in its handmade, naive quality. Cut the shapes freehand, rather than tracing them, to achieve a dynamic, spontaneous look.

YOU WILL NEED
- large sheet of watercolour paper
- scissors
- set of watercolour paints
- selection of watercolour brushes
- white china mixing palette or old white plate
- small piece of natural sponge
- large sheet of handmade paper
- picture frame
- design shapes (see page 157)
- fine black felt-tipped pen
- PVA (white) glue and brush *or* spray mount adhesive

1 *Cut the watercolour paper into small pieces. Using watercolour paints, spend at least an hour painting different patterns.*

2 *Use a sponge to add a different texture to some of the patterns.*

3 *Cut the handmade paper to fit the frame.*

4▷ *Paint a piece of watercolour paper plain green and fold in half. Using a felt-tipped pen, draw branch shapes, leaving a narrow space on the fold for the tree trunk. Follow the design shapes for reference. Cut out the branches, then open out the tree shape.*

➤

5 *Cut different flower shapes from your patterned papers.*

6 *Cut leaves, berries and birds the same way. Cut a base for the tree to sit on.*

7 *Glue the tree trunk and branches in the centre of the handmade paper.*

8 *Add the main flowers and the base of the tree.*

9 *Build up your own Tree of Life, adding all the other elements. Finally, add the birds. Fit the collage into the frame.*